M000014276

NURSERY RHYMES FOR BAD LITTLE CHILDREN

Adults Only

Product of KENNCO
13217 New Hampshire Avenue
#10908
Silver Spring, MD 20914
kennco33@gmail.com

US Copyright: 1-2005392881 Dec 2014
ISBN: 978-1-4951-4025-9

Acknowledgement to principal artist Laura-Leigh Palmer.
Artist Julia, assistance from Karen, Karl, Jana, Kaela,
Earle, Becky, J. Allen and the rest of the J's.

More Nursery Rhymes for Bad Little Children coming soon!

Price $14.95 + shipping/handling $2.05

TABLE OF CONTENTS

1 Georgie Porgie Pumpkin Pie 5
2 Hey Diddle Diddle 7
3 Humpty Dumpty 9
4 Jack and Jill 11
5 Jack B. Nimble 13
6 Little Bo Peep 15
7 Little Boy Blue 17
8 Little Jack Horner 19
9 Little Miss Muffet 21
10 Mary Had a Little Lamb 23
11 Mary, Mary Quite Contrary 25
12 Old Mother Hubbard 27
13 Old Woman Living In a Shoe 29
14 Old Man and The Shoe 31
15 Rock-a-Bye Baby 33
16 Song of Six-Pence 35
17 Star Light, Star Bright 37
18 Three Blind Mice 39
19 Three Little Kittens 41
20 Yankee Doodle 43

Georgie Porgie Pumpkin Pie

Georgie Porgie Pumpkin Pie

kissed the girls and

made them cry.

When Georgie Porgie came

out to play

all the girls just ran

away.

Cause Georgie Porgie

had the gift.

The gift that caused the rift.

Georgie had indeed been bad.

Cause herpes was the

gift he had.

2

Hey Diddle Diddle

Hey Diddle Diddle
the cat and the fiddle,
the cow jumped
over the moon.
Bull shit with that,
next you'll tell me
the dish ran away
with the spoon.

3

Humpty Dumpty

Humpty Dumpty sat on the wall
Humpty Dumpty had
a great fall.
The King said:
"If you think I'm
going to use all of
my horses and all
of my men
to put your clumsy
ass together again,
then think again,
you awkward mother –fucker!!"

4

Jack and Jill

Jack and Jill
went up the hill
to fetch a pail
of water.
Jack fell down
and broke his crown.
And Jill said:
"You're one clumsy
sum-bitch!!
And we still
don't have no water."

5

Jack B. Nimble

Jack be nimble.

Jack be quick.

Jack jumped over

the candle stick.

Jack didn't know

the wick was lit.

Jack done gone

and burned his dick!

Little Bo Peep

Little Bo Peep
had lost her sheep,
and didn't know
where to find them.
If the night-life
bitch
hadn't gone to sleep
she never would
have lost them!!

Little Boy Blue

Little Boy Blue
come blow your horn
so early in the morn.
First of all
it ain't no horn,
it's a got dammed
bugle!
You're in the Army!!
Now git your ass
out there
and sound *Reville*!!

Little Jack Horner

Little Jack Horner
sat in the corner
eating his
Christmas pie.
He stuck in his thumb
and pulled out a plum.
Then Jack said:
"Who put this friggin' fruit
in my sweet potato pie??"

Little Miss Muffet

Little Miss Muffet

sat on a tuffet

eating her curds

and whey.

Along came a spider

who sat down beside

her

and said:

"What you got in the bag bitch?"

Mary Had A Little Lamb

Mary had a little lamb
his fleece was white as snow.
Everywhere that Mary went
the Lamb was sure to go.
He followed her to school
one day,
they found Mary in the
family way.
Turns out that was no
lamb, but a ram.
You guessed it,
Mary had a little lamb!!

Mary. Mary Quite Contrary

Mary, Mary quite contrary

how does your garden

grow?

With silver bells

and cockell shells

all in a row.

We can't eat no

silver bells

and what the hell

are cockell shells?

Plant some beans

and corn, BITCH!

Old Mother Hubbard

Old Mother Hubbard

went to the cupboard

to get her dog a bone.

The cupboard was bare

so the hungry dog

bit Mother Hubbard

dead in the ASS!!

Old Woman Living In A Shoe

There was an old woman

who lived in a shoe.

She had so many children

she didn't know

what to do.

First, stop all that

sleeping around.

And second…

how about some birth control

bitch!!

Old Man and The Shoe

There was an Old Man
who lived near the shoe.
And I've heard it said
and the rumors were spread,
that the Old Man had been seen
coming out of the shoe,
deep in the morning
about half past two.
When confronted with this,
the Old man said:
"Old ladies ain't my bit
so don't go around spreading
that shit.
None of those kids
are in my family tree
So kiss my ass
don't pin it on me!"

15

Rock-a-Bye Baby

Rock-a-bye baby
in the tree top,
when the wind blows
the cradle will rock.
When the bough breaks
the cradle will fall.
Down will come baby
cradle and all.
Also down comes
the indictment,
for child abuse.
For putting baby
and cradle
up in the damned tree!

Song of Six-Pence

Sing a song of six-pence
pocket full of rye,
four and twenty black birds
baked in a pie.
When the pie was opened
the birds didn't fly.
Them wasn't no black birds
it was chicken pot pie
you silly asshole.

Star Light, Star Bright

Star light,

Star bright.

First star

I see tonight.

Way up in the

sky so high,

just like a fuckin'

eagle!

Three Blind Mice

Three blind mice
see how they run.
They all ran
after the farmer's
wife.
They got their tails
cut off with
a butcher knife.
"You thought I was
the farmers wife.
I'm just her friend
visiting from the city.
Next time you'll pay
with your damned life!"

Three Little Kittens

Three little kittens
had lost their mittens
and didn't know
where to find them.
Their mama said:
"You better git your
asses back outside
and find them.
Those fuckin' gloves
were expensive!"

Yankee Doodle

Yankee Doodle went

to town,

riding on a pony.

He stuck a feather

in his cap and

called it macaroni.

Now that's a bunch

of baloney.

"I'm not eatin' no

feathered hat,

even if you put marianara

and meatballs on it,

MUTHA-FUCKA."